Salvation
IS THE
EASIER
PART

Salvation
IS THE
EASIER
PART

*Writings and Illustrations
on Living the Christian Life*

JUDY KENT DAVIDSON

TATE PUBLISHING
AND ENTERPRISES, LLC

Published by Tate Publishing & Enterprises, LLC
127 E. Trade Center Terrace | Mustang, Oklahoma 73064 USA
1.888.361.9473 | www.tatepublishing.com

Tate Publishing is committed to excellence in the publishing industry. The company reflects the philosophy established by the founders, based on Psalm 68:11,
"The Lord gave the word and great was the company of those who published it."

Book design copyright © 2013 by Tate Publishing, LLC. All rights reserved.
Cover design by Jan Sunday Quilaquil
Interior design by Jomel Pepito

Published in the United States of America

ISBN: 978-1-62854-921-8
1. Religion / General
2. Religion / Christian Life / General
13.01.13

Dedication

This book is dedicated to my parents, Miriam and Charles Kent, and my husband, Don, for their lifelong love and support.

Contents

Illustrations

Gloria S. Toelle

Preface

This book has been a long time in the making. It started as just an idea many years ago in response to a need I had and saw all around me. Namely, people want to know how to daily walk with Jesus and need this information to be in simple, practical terms. It has been my observation that most folks would rather hear about our trials, frustrations, and even failures rather than our successes. Life is not a bowl of cherries and anyone who paints a Pollyanna view of the world cannot help those who are troubled.

I have many wonderful people in my life, each who has experienced various trials and each who has a story to tell. The writings here are true stories written by real people who want you to know how Jesus has walked with them through the years. They want you to know that life has mountaintops and valleys and all the places in between; and God knows exactly where you are at all times. They want you to know that Jesus has been, is now, and always will be with us. His Holy Spirit will help us with moment to moment decision making and is our counselor and guide.

It is my prayer that each person, who reads or hears these stories and views the illustrations, will find something uniquely placed just for him or her. We are all seekers. And Jesus has promised us that if we seek *him*, we will *find* him.

Salvation is the Easier Part

Judy K. Davidson

Dear Child of God, do you know and believe that Jesus is LORD? Spelled in all capitals, L-O-R-D is the divine name of YHWH (YAHWEH), Jehovah, and The I Am Who I AM. The LORD is the one and only Lord. The apostle Paul tells us that one day "every knee shall bow in heaven and on earth and under the earth, and every tongue will confess that Jesus Christ is Lord" (Philippians 2:9–11 RSV). *Every* is all inclusive—even Satan will bow and confess that Jesus is Lord!

So why does it matter if we serve the LORD or the Lord? I have observed that Christians readily call Jesus, Lord, but many confuse the meanings of *Savior* and *Lord*. How can these two concepts be distinguished in our minds? Let's look at Jesus as *Savior* first.

Understanding that we need salvation comes from a response to that spiritual hunger from within. We hear, read, and discuss that the way to heaven is by way of the cross. Each Christian comes to a point in which he or she is convicted of sin; the process of being convicted of sin and realizing that we are completely unable to help ourselves, leads to the understanding that we need a Savior. If we then confess our sins and ask for forgiveness, we will receive salvation. The Bible plainly The Bible plainly states, "if you confess with your mouth, 'Jesus is Lord,' and believe in your heart that God raised him from the dead, you will be saved" (Romans 10:9 NIV). This is the *Good News* or *gospel* and is true. The Good News reveals to us that our salvation comes by way of grace—the unmerited favor of God. The decision to ask for forgiveness and salvation is arguably the most important decision we will ever make.

Christians, then, are persons who have recognized and believed Jesus. We are changed but we retain our humanity and self-centeredness. Self-preservation necessitates a degree of self-care. Our journey from infancy to adulthood should properly move from being the "center of the universe" to being concerned with the welfare of others. Our spiritual journey should equally lead to such growth.

Salvation is a uniquely personal event: I am a sinner—I have been disobedient—I must confess my sin—I have to ask for forgiveness—and I must plan to lead a different life. No other human can in any way purchase my passage to heaven. Only I can ask for me and only God can grant forgiveness and salvation. *Good people* don't go to heaven; *saved people* go.

So, up to this point, salvation is all about Jesus and me. I could go live on a deserted island with my Bible and be happy as a clam. I am saved and since works don't buy my ticket to heaven, I'm done. How self-satisfied—how Western—how smug—and what an immature view of the Christian journey! And I must confess to you that this once was my understanding of the Christian Life. Thankfully, God is still working on me and continues giving me wisdom as I am able to grasp it.

Now let us ponder Jesus as LORD. Brothers and Sisters, Jesus is God. God is the omnipotent, omniscient, sovereign, immutable Creator. He was, is, and forever will be. He is *love*, *truth*, *mercy*, *justice*, and *light*. He is *life*. We were made in his image for his glory. This is his world and his plan. And his plan is that we who are his disciples go into the world he made and bring other people to him.

This concept of bringing others to God takes the process beyond our personal salvation. If we allow Jesus to truly be

Lord or Master of our lives, then it follows that we are his servants. What does a servant do? A true servant is the one who is ready and willing to do what the *master* commands. This servant doesn't whine or complain or ask why someone else doesn't have to do the work. In other words, a true servant is *obedient*.

Jesus told his disciples that "the one who loves him is the one who obeys him; and the one who obeys him is the one who loves him" (John 14:15, 21, NIV). So you see, the reason I say that *salvation* is the easier part is because it is a one-time event. Obedience is the harder part. If we only had to take up our cross *once* and suffer *once*, that would be heroic—another thing to be *proud* about. Daily cross bearing is a whole different proposition because it is so constant. Be honest—in the beginning of our Christian walk don't we really want to do that one great thing, be finished, and go back to being ourselves? This is because we know that if we truly acknowledge Jesus as our Lord and behave as committed disciples, we will have to make permanent changes.

As with many things spiritual, this obedience thing is a paradox. We are commanded to be obedient but we can only be obedient through the guidance of and help of the Holy Spirit. Our Lord invites us to be yoked with him wearing that harness he has crafted to exactly fit each of us.

He wants us to be vigilant and pay attention to what he is doing. As we spend time with him daily reading his word and praying, he speaks to us through his Holy Spirit. As we grow spiritually, we learn to hear, feel, trust, and obey the Spirit's guidance. And we learn that while obedience is surely a constant thing, it also is so sweet. The obedient servant is the one who can truly call Jesus both *Savior and LORD.*

The following essays are written from the heart by fellow Christians who know Jesus. I invite you to read their stories and hear their affirmations. The illustrations are filled with love and peace. I encourage you to study them slowly and pray the scriptures that accompany each painting.

Room for One More

Larry Coger

I grew up in a small southern town in east Alabama. Like many southern cities and towns everything was centered around the textile mills. The war was over, Elvis had arrived on the scene singing "You Ain't Nothing but a Hound Dog", and life seemed simple and carefree. My family lived a few miles outside of town on the Water Works Road, but when a developer started a subdivision on the main highway into town, my family decided to build a house in this new style of residential development. The proximity of the houses gave new meaning to the word neighbors. The houses were a lot closer than those on the main highway, so it took some time to get used to having people live next door.

On the main road into the town next to where the

subdivision's main entrance was located, there was a church. The members of the church were excited about the new subdivision. They visited throughout the community on Wednesday nights to invite people to come and worship with them. Since the houses were so close together, the members could walk door to door in the neighborhood and visit instead of having to drive from house to house along the main road. When they came to visit our house, my mother was glad to see them. We never had many visitors at our old house. My mother knew many of the visitors from her workplace at the mill. She decided that we should begin to attend church; so on Sunday my older sister, younger brother, and I went to church for the first time.

My stepfather refused to go. I don't know why, except in retrospect, I suspect it was his pride that kept him from going. He knew many of the people from work at the mill also. My relationship with my stepfather was never very good. We had little in common and since I and the rest of the family were attending church, the relationship became even more distant. He had no children of his own and had never learned any parenting skills. To him and for far too many other men of the era, parenting meant providing food, shelter, clothing, and transportation. Being a good parent equated to being a good provider for your children until they could provide for themselves.

In spite of my stepfather's refusal to go, my mother, being the persistent woman that she was, took my brother, sister, and me to church each Sunday. I felt an immediate attraction to the people and the activities at the church. I was nine years old at the time. I enjoyed Sunday School, Training Union on Sunday night, and prayer meeting on Wednesday night, but what I enjoyed the most was Vacation Bible School during the summer. There was always something going on for the youth group. We played baseball, basketball, fished, and swam. We went on picnics and enjoyed a few hayrides. The atmosphere was one of love and caring for me as a young person. In retrospect I have realized that what attracted me to the church were the very things I wanted and needed at home. Romans 8:28 was in effect then and to this day remains one of my favorite lessons from the Bible. "And we know that in all things God works for the good of those who love him, who have been called according to his purpose." (NIV)

After attending church for two years and at the age of eleven, I began to be constantly aware of a void, an empty spot within me, that I did not understand. Something within me was yearning for meaning and purpose. I was only eleven years old, but mind you, I was by necessity a mature eleven-year-old.

The lessons and examples of the pastor, Sunday School teachers, and Vacation Bible School teachers helped me recognize that the feelings that I was experiencing were the call of the Holy Spirit to come by faith and to trust Jesus as my savior. I prayed one night to Jesus and admitted that I was a sinner and asked him to come into my life. He did so that night. Then came the hard part where I had to make my decision known to my pastor, my family, and all the people in the church. I must admit that I prayed to Jesus many times asking that we keep this one decision just between us.

After a period of agonizing over the event, I made my decision known and to my surprise everyone was happy about it. I had feared that they would be judgmental and question my age and experience to make such a monumental decision. I also had a deep fear of expressing my deepest emotions in public. It has taken almost a lifetime to conquer this fear. But the decision had been made, made public, and I can't begin to tell you how relieved I was. That empty void within me was filled and I felt an inner peace that was beyond my understanding. In retrospect, I now realize that this was the most critical point in my life. A point where a decision, a commitment, made or not made established the path for the rest of my life. I had no idea at the time how much it would mean to me for Christ to be the guiding hand in my life journey.

When I was fifteen years old, I desperately needed a job. I had worked for my stepfather assembling aluminum screens and building screen porches. One of my assignments was to paint the screen porch frame prior to placing the screen cloth. Since I had some experience painting, I approached a man at church about a job. James worked at the mill from 6:00 a.m. until 2:00 p.m. After work, he painted houses in the afternoons and on Saturdays. James said he could use some help, but I would have to start out doing prep work like scraping the old paint off and sanding. I agreed to $0.50 per hour and James said that he would pick me up at my house the next day on his way to the job site. I was determined to prove my worth and earn James' approval. My effort was soon rewarded and James let me start painting as well as doing the prep work. He gave me a raise up to $1.00 per hour. It was sufficient for me to provide the things that I needed.

Our employee/employer relationship grew to much more over the years to a friendship that approached a father/son relationship. James became in my eyes that which I desired to be as a husband and father. He didn't preach or teach me with words about life's priorities, but he lived them in such a way that I understood them clearly. His faith in God, though not often spoken about, was clearly his top priority. His family was second and he always put his needs and wants last. He was a humble man and always put those around him before himself. He had two sons and a daughter whom he loved as much as any father could. He was driven by a commitment to them to provide the things they needed to enjoy life and to prepare themselves to be successful.

We spent many hours working side by side painting houses. We talked about life in general. We pretty much had solved all the problems in the world and couldn't understand why everyone didn't recognize the truths we understood so clearly. James had fought in WW II. He was part of the Normandy invasion and advanced through France to Germany. He wouldn't talk about the war very much. He always said that it was in the past and best left there. He did say that the Allies came very close to losing the war while he was in France. Of the few war stories he would tell, the ride home on the Queen Mary was his favorite. I suppose it was because the war was over and the site of home soil was so precious. I learned a lot of life lessons from James. One thing he taught me was that no matter what the circumstances or how busy life seemed, enjoy the moment you find yourself in.

One beautiful sunny Saturday morning found us finishing a job in Meadow Cliff Subdivision. It was a lovely neighborhood with a street down both sides of a brook. We only lacked painting the front and back screen doors with black paint. While we were opening the can of black paint, our competitor drove slowly by the house we were painting. He had a nice new truck with a ladder rack on the back. There wasn't a splotch of paint anywhere on that truck—very neat and clean. On each of the doors there was a sign that read O. E. Gray House Painting with the phone number listed below the name. James commented on what a nice looking truck it was and wondered aloud why he was riding around instead of working. I acknowledged the subtle comment and headed to the back of the house to paint the screen door. It was Saturday morning and I was excited by the thought that we might finish the job by lunch and not start another job until Monday, which would give me an afternoon off.

I finished the back door and headed back to the front of the house to clean up and get everything put up and ready to go. I stopped in my tracks as I approached the old green Buick we called the paint wagon. James was painting a sign on the side of the Buick with the brush and black paint he was supposed to be using on the front door. Now you have to understand that the green Buick

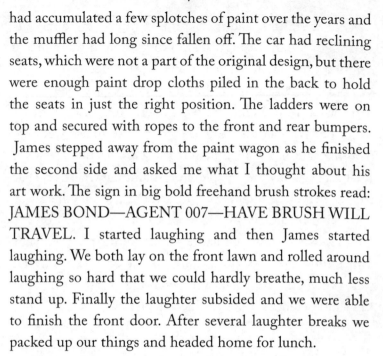

had accumulated a few splotches of paint over the years and the muffler had long since fallen off. The car had reclining seats, which were not a part of the original design, but there were enough paint drop cloths piled in the back to hold the seats in just the right position. The ladders were on top and secured with ropes to the front and rear bumpers. James stepped away from the paint wagon as he finished the second side and asked me what I thought about his art work. The sign in big bold freehand brush strokes read: JAMES BOND—AGENT 007—HAVE BRUSH WILL TRAVEL. I started laughing and then James started laughing. We both lay on the front lawn and rolled around laughing so hard that we could hardly breathe, much less stand up. Finally the laughter subsided and we were able to finish the front door. After several laughter breaks we packed up our things and headed home for lunch.

As we drove through the downtown district, people stopped, stared, pointed at the paint wagon and began laughing. We really had everybody's attention and decided that we had stumbled upon a very good advertising gimmick. We were beaming with pride as we drove up the hill to James' house with great anticipation for a fine lunch Mrs. B would surely have prepared. I saw Mrs. B. peeking out the kitchen window as we drove up. I do declare that from that window, Mrs. B could figure out just about anything going on in the world. She seemed to have built-in "radar" that enabled her to know when something was up. On this day she came out the back door drying her hands on her apron and started pointing at the green Buick paint wagon. Needless to say she wasn't nearly as proud of our handiwork as we were. She ranted for several minutes about what we had done. The conversation contained the word *fool* numerous times and to my dismay the word *fools* was used multiple times. James calmed Mrs. B down and told me to take the green Buick to my house. I knew what to do. I took some mineral spirits and washed James' sign off. When I drove the green Buick back up the hill to James' house, Mrs. B. was looking out that window again. She came out, looked at my corrective procedures, and started laughing. The lunch was great.

Christmas was a special time of the year for James and Mrs. B. They loved to give gifts to their children and share great family time surrounding the finest Christmas dinners ever prepared. They were careful to celebrate the birth of Jesus at Christmas and to extend that celebration to their family and friends. The right Christmas tree was very important to Mrs. B. and as the Christmas season approached one year, she reminded James that he needed to find a tree so she could get started with the decorations. Mrs. B was a highly energetic woman and didn't like to wait until the last minute to do anything. There were very few trees for sale on the corner or at the hardware store during the season since most people had property or had access to family property with cedar trees, which were plentiful in the area and were the preferred tree. While we were eating lunch one Saturday, Mrs. B. reminded James again that he needed to find a tree! James and I looked at one another and we both knew what the other was thinking. "We'll take care of it," James assured Mrs. B. As we prepared to leave for the job site after lunch, I slipped a small cross cut saw in the back of the station wagon. The green Buick had finally died and was now a storage vehicle for all the painting paraphernalia. The previous family car, a white station wagon, was now the painting business vehicle, having been replaced by a new Impala. It was a nice vehicle, but lacked the character of the green Buick by a long shot.

James and I had been eyeing a cedar tree on the bank above the new four lane road that led toward the downtown area. We had decided that the tree was just outside the fence that marked the property line and was surely on the right of way, which was public property. We had decided that we were qualified members of the public and that the tree needed to be harvested before it became too large. We worked late that Saturday and it was almost dark when we headed home. James eased the station wagon over to the side of the road just below the embankment where the cedar tree was located. I grabbed the saw and up the bank we went.

That bank was a good bit higher and steeper than we thought, but we managed to reach the tree. I hurriedly cut the tree at its base just above the ground. We each grabbed a bottom limb and down the bank we went. We shoved the tree into the back of the station wagon, jumped in, and scattered a little gravel as we took off. We laughed all the way home. We unloaded the tree and placed it on the front porch. Mrs. B. came out and commented on what a nice tree it was.

James retrieved the tree stand from the shed and we mounted it on the base of the tree. We stood the tree up and carried it through the front door into the living room. It was then that we realized that the tree was a little taller than we had estimated while observing it on our trips in and out of town. Mrs. B. said something that contained the words fool and fools again. Not a problem, James declared as we took the tree back to the front porch, cut off about two feet, and mounted it in the stand once more. We took the tree inside and to my amazement the tree top was just below the ceiling—perfect. I don't believe James ever owned a measuring tape. He just looked at things and seemed to know the length.

However, Mrs. B. noted a problem. It seems that the branches on a cedar tree start at the bottom and extend quite a distance up the tree. When we cut two feet off the bottom, it left quite a void of limbs half way up the tree. Mrs. B. declared the tree to be the ugliest tree that she had ever seen and that it just wouldn't do. James declared that it would have to do, to which Mrs. B declared; "All right, I know what to do." I grabbed a hand full of door knob and headed home!

About a week later I learned what Mrs. B. meant by her declaration. I walked into the living room and there was the tree with beautifully wrapped packages stacked around it almost to the top and cascading down to the floor in a perfect Christmas tree cone shape. There was no way to determine what the bottom two thirds of that tree looked like. I started to laugh and even though I tried to hide my laughter, Mrs. B. knew what I was thinking. She said she appreciated James and I taking those bottom limbs off so she could have more room.

It was the evening of Christmas day and I had been invited to have Christmas dinner with James and his family. When I arrived they presented me with a gift from beneath the tree. The other packages had all been opened and the wrapping paper and boxes now filled the area around the tree. I smiled inside again as I opened my gift.

As we sat around the dining room table, I surveyed what was likely the finest Christmas dinner ever prepared. There was turkey, ham, dressing, cranberry sauce, vegetables of every kind, gravy and every desert that anyone had ever mentioned that they liked. As James gave thanks for our meal, I thanked God that James and his family had included me in their celebration. I thanked God for the friendship of James and Christine (Mrs. B.); and for Jimmy, Jeffery, and Margaret's willingness to share their family time with me.

I came across the word *influencers* recently. An influence is defined as something or someone that has an indirect effect. Thus, an influencer is a person who has an indirect effect on other people. The word was used to describe Christians and the effect they have on people around them, even though they may not be cognizant of the influence. I believe that God uses influencers more than we realize to accomplish his work in the lives of those who trust him. As I look back, I clearly recognize that the Wednesday night visitors, Sunday school teachers, youth directors, pastors, and Vacation Bible School teachers were influencers in my life and used by God to lead me to him. God has placed many more influencers in my life since that time, probably more than I could ever remember or recognize. I am certain that one of the ways that God placed his guiding hand on me was through James and his family. I was thankful as I sat at the table that night at Christmas many years ago and remain grateful to this day that they found room at their table and in their hearts for one more.

Heavenly Father,

As I contemplate my life's journey, I see your guiding hand on my life.

There have been many forks in the road. There have been many opportunities for my journey to depart from your plan for my life. Thank you for your guiding hand that has kept my journey on the right path.

I can now see how you have used other people to minister to me. Some led me to salvation in my youth. Others have ministered to me along my journey. I praise your holy name for your guiding hand and owe a debt of gratitude to those who were willing to be used by you.

Now, help me to recognize and respond to your call to be used by you to minister to others. I feel great joy when your spirit works through me. Thank you for that joy.

Thank you Lord for your Holy Spirit who dwells in me and works through me. Renew your spirit in me this day. May all praise, glory, and honor be to your holy name.

Amen

My Testimony

Judy K. Davidson

There once was a girl who was born in the late 1940s, went to grammar school in the 50s and high school and college in the 60s. She married in the late 60s just prior to her senior year in college. She graduated, went to work for a while, and then went on to graduate school. She and her husband moved to Columbus, Georgia after graduation and began their careers. In 1972 they had their first child, a beautiful baby boy.

Up until this point, her life had resembled the old TV series, "Father Knows Best." Her parents loved God, each other, and all four of their children. They made church and worshiping God a priority in the family life. Both parents and all four children went to Sunday School and church on Sunday mornings and back to church Sunday evening. The children all went to Bible School, summer church camp, and youth group when old enough. They were economically poor by today's standards but did not know it. In spite of financial difficulties, the parents sent all four children to college. All four graduated and two have master's degrees. The parents taught their children right from wrong and taught them that there really are absolutes in this world. They set a good example for Godly living and the girl learned early on to love and trust the Lord.

In 1972, after giving birth to the child she and her husband had so longed for, her world turned upside down. It was necessary for her to go back to work when the baby was only five weeks old. She developed a deep depression—a post-partum depression—that sent her spiraling down into a dark, cold, horrible place. She was miserable and hated almost everyone and everything she had to do. She thought about suicide every day. She knew where her husband kept his gun and thought about using it many times.

Her husband and mother tried to help her but did not know how. The young woman met their attempts to understand her feelings with anger. Her only reason for living was the baby. You see, she had learned in growth and development courses that children, whose mothers committed suicide, always blamed themselves. She could not let her little boy grow up believing that something about him was not good enough or that his mother had not loved him enough to live.

All through this time, the woman was going to church sporadically. A new Sunday School class was created named *TNT* or Teachers in Training. This class was designed to prepare persons to teach children and adult Sunday School classes. She was invited to attend this class and finally said yes when it was offered the second time in 1974.

God is good. During this time, He had led the pastor to preach a series of sermons about spiritual growth and then had the facilitator of the TNT class pose this question. She said, "Suppose your spiritual life can be compared to being present at the Sermon on the Mount where Jesus was teaching while standing in a boat. Where are you: in the boat with Jesus, on the shore wading in the water, or on the bank just watching and listening?" In her heart, the young woman knew she was on the bank. Now that may not seem like a monumental question and answer session to you, but it started a catharsis in her life that melted the ice around her heart and had her answer an altar call to rededicate her life to the Lord.

She began a daily devotional time and found several Psalms written by David and others that spoke directly to her heart and could have been penned by her:

> I waited patiently for the Lord. He turned to me and heard my cry. He lifted me out of the pit of

destruction, out of sticky mud. He stood me on a rock and made my feet steady. He put a new song in my mouth, a song of praise to our God.

Psalm 40:1-3
(NCV)

I love the Lord, because he listens to my prayers for help. He paid attention to me, so I will call to him for help as long as I live. The ropes of death bound me; the fear of the grave took hold of me. I was troubled and sad. Then I called out the name of the Lord. I said, 'Please, Lord, save me!'

...Lord, you saved me from death. You stopped my eyes from crying and you kept me from being defeated. So I will walk with the Lord in the land of the living.

Psalm 116: 1-4, 8-9
(NCV)

I was in trouble, so I called to the Lord. The Lord answered me and set me free. I will not be afraid, because the Lord is with me. People can't do anything to me. The Lord is with me to help me, so I will see my enemies defeated.

Psalm 118:5-7
(NCV)

As I am sure you have guessed, I was that girl and young woman. I have used the third person approach up until this point in my story because the girl before the TNT class is gone. In her place is a new creation. Was I spiritually dead or just asleep? Only God knows. What I do know is that my conscious spiritual journey began with that class. I slowly learned to be a disciple. I learned to mine the scriptures for truth and promises. I have built my life on the solid rock of Jesus. I have been convinced by the Holy Spirit that my name is in the Book of Life, not because I have ever done anything to deserve it, but because of *grace*. I have learned that where I am weak, God is strong. I know that *he* is willing and able to plan my life and weave me into the fabric of his plan for *his honor* and *glory*. I know that I can *trust* Jesus.

Did you notice all those sentences that began with "I" in the paragraph you just read? So did God. Remember that I told you God is good? One blessed day my sister in Christ, Betty, asked me if I would consider being an Emmaus pilgrim; I told her I was just too busy. Then my dear friend, Ann, went on her Emmaus walk and told me what a tremendous experience it was. And I began to think seriously about being a pilgrim.

God orchestrated the perfect time for me and I went in October 2005 sponsored by Betty and Ann. This was a particularly hectic time in my life and I really did not have any time to think about my Walk. Emmaus persons in my church would ask, "Are you excited about your Walk?" I would truthfully answer that I had not even thought about it. In fact, it occurred to me that I was crazy to go away for four days when I had so much to do.

That weekend a whirlwind of emotions and spiritual growth engulfed me. Looking back on this very important time in my life, I can say that the Lord saturated my mind with these two things:

1. He loves me perfectly and completely just as I am. I am *his* child and, as such, I don't have to be good enough in any way. Since nothing can separate me from the love of God expressed through Christ Jesus, I don't have to worry that something I do will make me lose my place in the family of God.

2. There is an enormous amount of pain in this world and no one is immune from it. All of us have experienced pain, some are experiencing pain right now, and all of us will experience pain in the future. Pain can be either physical, emotional, spiritual or some combination of all three. It can be caused from many sources and is often hidden from sight. God told me to open my eyes and see and care about *his* hurting people all around me.

Since that weekend, my whole outlook has changed. How I wish I could tell you that I am a completely changed person who never misses the opportunity to ease another's cares. I wish I could say that; but the truth is that God and I continue working towards this goal. Every day I ask God to help me don the full armor of Christ and then ask him to be my vision, my hearing, think my thoughts, speak my words, and guide my feet for I don't want to walk this way in vain. And he has increased my awareness so very much. He has given me many opportunities to tell people how much he loves them and how he is willing and able to help them. He has shown me that *people* are precious to him—not my plans.

My approach to life can now be summed up with lines from two of my favorite hymns:

> And since He bids me seek His face, believe His word, and trust His grace, I'll cast on Him my every care and wait for thee, sweet hour of prayer.
>
> *Sweet Hour of Prayer*,
> William W. Walford, 1845.

> Every day they pass me by; I can see it in their eyes. Lonely people filled with care, who knows what or where? On they go in private pain, living fear to fear. Who can hear their silent cries? Only Jesus hears. People need the Lord; people need the Lord.

At the end of broken dreams, He's the open door.
People need the Lord; people need the Lord. When
will we realize, people need the Lord?

People Need the Lord,
Gregory A. Nelson and Phillip McHugh, 1983.

Dear Father,

*Just like the psalmist, I was in trouble; so I called out
to you. You heard me, and answered me and set me
free. I will praise your name and tell others about your
wonderful love and care as long as I have breath. You
are mine and I am yours; I am complete. Please accept
my forever gratitude. Amen.*

Staying within the Lines

Chuck Bradshaw

School teachers do it. Sunday School teachers do it. I'll bet you've had it done to you. And if you're a parent, you probably have done it to your children. Can you recall the first time, long ago, when someone handed you a few crayons along with a piece of paper bearing the outline of a simple object or animal and gave you instructions to color it? Do you recall the final words of the instruction? "Be sure to stay within the lines!" When we did so, we were rewarded with praise. When we transgressed, we were admonished regarding the purposes of lines and encouraged to try to do better the next time. Chances are that we do the same to those in our charge.

As I learned to stay within the lines, being careful not to mix my colors, I eventually graduated to paint-by-number sets—cardboard covered with canvas upon which lines are printed. Inside those lines are numbers that correspond to numbers on the enclosed paints. Instructions are simple enough. Match the number on the paint vial to the number on the canvas. Seldom did my final rendition resemble the likeness on the cover of the box. I had become so adept at *not* transgressing the lines that none of my various colors of paint even contacted each other. The worst experience, however, was when, on occasion, the manufacturer would fail to place a number in an area. What was I to do? Though my efforts of seeking to reproduce a masterpiece worthy of hanging usually fell short, nevertheless I always was praised for my ability to stay within the lines.

Among the first lessons the Bible teaches is that humanity was made in the image of God. Since God is spirit, the image we bear has nothing to do with height, weight and color of eyes. Rather, we are like God in that we can reason, we can feel, we can make choices, we have the faculty of speech and, believe it or not, we have creativity. When God placed man in the primeval garden, he assigned him the role of caretaker. Nowhere does the Bible report that God told our ancient ancestor *how* to garden. Man had a mind. God expected man to use his wits and his creativity. Recall also that God brought the animals to the man and told *him* to name them. What freedom! How wonderful to be all that God intended for him to be—living creatively for the glory of God.

Trouble came to Paradise when man decided to go his own way. The result was that God's image was distorted. Our primeval parents used their creativity to blame others. "It was the *woman* that *You* gave me," said the man. In spite of their evasive actions, God sought them out. He clothed their nakedness with the skin of an animal—an innocent animal whose life was forfeited for the sake of that guilty couple. The rest of the Old Testament is a history of human plotting and strategizing in order to try to control circumstances and other people. It is a record of people seeking, by any means, to make other people stay within the lines. Interspersed are promises of the One coming who would restore God's image to his people. With that restoration would come a freedom to be creative—to break out of the lines drawn by others —truly free to be what God intended. Then the Lord Jesus Christ came!

One would think that the message of real freedom would be welcomed. Yet the message of freedom cost Jesus his life. People tend to become uncomfortable when those around them begin to cross the lines that they have drawn. All of us tend to assign roles to others. As long as they follow the assigned script and cues, everything is fine. All their efforts are applauded. How wonderfully we stay within the lines

—lines that someone else has drawn! The gospel of the free grace of God in Christ is like ink eradicator that renders the canvas free of numbers and lines. Then God says, "Live creatively." That kind of freedom is intimidating to people accustomed only to coloring within the lines of someone else's drawing.

But what of God's sovereignty? Doesn't God have a plan and purpose for every life? Is it not true that "all the days ordained for me were written in *your* book before one of them came to be" (Psalm 139:16 NIV)? Of course, it is true! God provides us with the materials for our creative use. The paper or canvas he gives us is of the dimensions of *his* choosing. None of us know the length—or brevity— of our days on earth. Those parameters are his prerogative. But God, as the wise Father he is, and unlike so many of us, does not pass out paper with bold-lined objects printed thereon and a couple of crayons and tell us to stay within the lines. No, God gives us a blank sheet and dumps out a whole box of crayons. He tells us that he loves us and that his desire for us is that we love him and love others— and, all the time, become more and more like his Son, the Lord Jesus. Then he tells us to choose the crayons that are available to us and to be creative for his glory.

Conformity to Christ's image does not mean that someday all of us will have brown eyes and a beard and be able to turn water into wine. The Bible speaks of God's people as new creations, not clones. God is not in the *copy machine* business. Reading the Bible should convince anyone of that. Consider the characters of the Bible. David and Deborah, John and Jonah, Paul and Priscilla, Thomas and Timothy were all true believers. Yet, how different were their personalities, their ministries and their spheres of influence. Each of them lived creatively, some filling their "canvas" with bold heavy strokes while others drew lightly in pastels. As God goes about his work of restoring his image in fallen, fallible people, part of that restoration is granting us the desire and ability to live creatively for the glory of God. He sets us free, not to copy the work of others nor to fill in lines drawn by others but, rather, to live original lives. Eugene Peterson wrote:

> That means we will not compare ourselves with each other as if one were better and another worse. We have far more interesting things to do with our lives. Each of us is an original. Live creatively, friends.... Make a careful exploration of who you are and the work you have been given, and then sink yourselves into that. Don't live vicariously. Each of us must take responsibility for doing the creative best we can with our own lives.

> *Traveling Light.*
> H & H Pub., 1988, pp. 163–164

How creative do we feel? Perhaps it's time to try something unconventional. After years of stifling our creativity, it is hard to believe that we *can* live creatively. Yet, we can. Forgiving others when they wrong us is creative. Speaking a kind word, listening attentively, extending a gentle touch, offering a helping hand—all these are creative ways to live. The neighborhoods of our community and the offices in the marketplace can serve as art galleries where the grace of God is displayed through us as we seek to live creatively for the glory of God and his Son, the Lord Jesus Christ. But mind you, it never will happen if we insist on staying within the lines.

Green Lights

Judy K. Davidson

Edwin Grimes was the first pastor of our United Methodist Church which was founded in 1927. After a long career in the ministry, he and his wife, Mildred, returned to Columbus as *retired* ministers. In their 80s and early 90s, Edwin and Mildred worked on various volunteer activities such as the food bank, visiting the sick, delivering meals to the homebound, and whatever the church leadership asked them to do.

Edwin was older than Mildred and as the years went by, she became their driver. As you might expect, she was not exactly a speed demon. One Sunday evening I attended a Bible study on *prayer* and Edwin was one of the participants. During a discussion he said," Mildred and I are sort of slow and often we run behind on some of our outings. Whenever I think we might be late, I just ask the Lord to give us green lights. Usually he does." From that day forward I have prayed for green lights, too. I figured that Edwin had been talking to God for many years and he knew a lot about answered prayers.

I have to confess that I too often run late. Not because I am slow—but because I try to do too much at home, at work, etc., before leaving. Oftentimes my prayers go like this, "Dear Lord, it is me again. You know I have underestimated how long it would take me to do (whatever) and did not give myself enough time to get (wherever) on time. If it is okay with you, may I please have green lights?" Just like Edwin, I have experienced that traffic lights turn green just as I am approaching them. And if they don't, I surmise that God is just protecting me from an accident. As a result, I too tell others to pray for green lights. Often folks are skeptical and say something like, "I am not going to pray about something that insignificant. God has more to do than give me green lights." I ask if the person has read in 1 Peter where it says, "Let him have all your worries and cares, for he is always thinking about you and watches everything that concerns you"(1 Peter 5:7, TLB). *Everything* includes green lights. And God can do anything and everything and all at once. He is not a human who has to prioritize and/or budget his time.

A few months ago I was in our room over the garage exercising with a yoga DVD. The phone rang and I considered not answering. Something made me pick up the phone and I heard, "Judy, this is Reed. I couldn't think of anyone else to call who lives close to me. I am having chest pain and am about to faint." I told him to hang up and call 911. Then he said," We don't have 911 out here." There I was at home alone, wearing my exercise clothes, and it was late in the afternoon. Reed is one of my husband's co-workers, and he lives about 25 miles away from us and in the opposite direction of the hospital. His house is sort of in the middle of nowhere off of several poorly marked dirt roads. In a flash I told him I would come get him and asked for directions; I had been to his house a couple of times but not in recent memory. I scribbled down directions and thought I would just use my GPS. *Au contraire*. When I typed in Reed's address, my GPS said "unable to find".

I drove as fast as possible to where I had to turn off the highway and thankfully the first road was paved. He had told me that I would pass a church and then turn onto John Creel Road. There was the church but no John Creel Road. I called him and *No Service* was what my trusty phone said. It was getting close to dusk and those street signs were very hard to read. I backtracked and saw a sign that said Jonquil Road; I finally realized that Reed's Creole accent made jonquil sound like John Creel. Now, I was finally on the right (dirt) road and miraculously my cell phone worked. He directed me through the rabbit warren of roads and I finally drove up into his front yard.

Out of his front door came Reed, a giant of a man. His color was awful—gray—and he was gasping for breath. He got into the car and I knew that I would never be able to move him out and perform CPR if it were necessary. He directed me out of the maze and we were back on the highway pretty fast. Now I was going to get on the Expressway and knew I would come to at least twelve traffic lights. You have to know I had been praying all along but now I added a request for *Green Lights*. I also drove as fast as I safely could all the while hoping that a policeman would see us and give us an escort to the ER. I never saw a policeman, but we didn't need one—every light turned green as we approached. I didn't even have to slow down. We pealed into the ER entrance and I ran inside to get help. The rest is history: Reed got the help he needed. He calls me his angel, but I tell him that all the glory and praise goes to God. He was the one who provided the green lights and kept Reed alive and able to talk to me on the phone.

I told this story to my Sunday School class a while back and several of my previously skeptical friends have started praying for green lights. Guess what? They tell me that when they pray for green lights, green lights they get.

Dear Heavenly Father,

You always listen to our prayers even if they are just one or two words. Thank you for being so interested and involved in our lives. You have promised that you will always be with us, always care about our worries and concerns, and always and forever love us. What a promise-keeper you are! Thank you for your faithfulness. As always, I pray in the name of your son and my savior, Jesus. Amen

Praise Him Anyway

Janet K. Cavin

What began as an ordinary Friday in July would prove to be one of the most extraordinary days of my life. I woke up that morning the same person I had been for forty-six years, but I would be completely different by lunchtime. I heard news on that day that I can only describe as life altering. It was news of betrayal, secrets, and abuse. I remember thinking, "This cannot be happening to *my* family!" But, sadly, it was happening and I feared I did not have the strength to face it. Alone I could not have ever made it through, but with God all things are possible.

Over the next few months, I would have to look at the reality of who my family was. As a pastor, many people had shared terrible truths about their own families. Often, as tales of infidelity and addictions were spoken, they would say, "I didn't know." I would think to myself at times that it was hard to believe they did not know a child was addicted to drugs or a spouse was unfaithful. I know now that there are secrets buried so deep and lies so cleverly crafted that it *is* possible not to know what is happening to those closest to you. My own experience was a parent's worst nightmare: my child had been hurt and I did not know. Anger, fear and confusion were only a few of the emotions I felt daily. I was consumed. In just a few short weeks, I lost my marriage, my job, and was forced to move. My family's crisis was made public and the Church itself seemed to be the enemy. It was all a terrible dream that I could not awaken from. In every sense of the word, I felt abandoned.

I would discover, however, that God had not abandoned us. In fact, he was always close, always providing. The church as the body of Christ would take on a deeper, richer, more mature meaning than ever before. Every day, and I mean *every day*, people would call on the phone, write letters, send e-mails, give money and pray for us. We were never alone. Through these people of faith, God provided a new job, an apartment, and money to pay the bills. Each day brought tangible expressions of God's faithfulness and love. When I felt I could not go on, God would send someone to provide the hope and encouragement needed for that particular day.

One morning the following spring, I woke up and realized that this crisis was not going to kill me and that I needed to look toward the future. I was still feeling lost and unsure. Often I would wake up in the night with a feeling of terror and emptiness. I told my sister, Judy, how I was feeling hoping she would have some wisdom to share and she suggested I praise God anyway no matter how I was feeling. She told me to praise him for all he had done and would do in our lives. So I began to do that daily. Each time I would feel afraid or lonely or uncertain I would praise and thank God for all the blessings we had received, for all the people whose love had sustained us, and for all the miracles he was providing.

About this same time a friend of mine, Kristi, called one day to say God had impressed on her spirit to tell me to pray for what he had put on my heart. As soon as she said this, I immediately knew what she was talking about. A few days before a very clear thought came to me. What I wanted more than anything was for a Godly, righteous man to love me and my children right where we were. I began to pray that prayer every day all the while praising God for all he had done and would do in our lives.

While praying the prayer for the Godly, righteous man, who would love me and my children right where we were to come into our lives, I began to look around at the men in my life. Sometimes I would think, "Surely not him Lord!" At one point I was sure I had prayed myself into marrying a missionary and would be moving all of us halfway around the world. A few months later, however, God would place in my path an old friend. His wife had died of cancer after suffering with that disease for sixteen years. My eyes were opened to seeing this old friend in a completely new light. He was a Godly, righteous man, but was he the answer to my prayer? I began to pray more fervently and specifically for God's guidance basically asking him, "Is this the man for whom I have been praying?" I felt God's response as a "yes" at every turn. Six months later we were married.

My husband, Mike, is another tangible expression of God's love for me and for my children. Additionally, through him, God has provided someone for me and my children to love; I have three new stepchildren to love and a new avenue in which to serve God's people and the Church. I believe God provided all this and more, in large part, through two Godly and faithful women, who encouraged me to praise God anyway and to follow the desires God placed in my heart.

Another good friend, Caroline, gave me a scripture verse to count on when life seemed at its worst and it still provides me with strength and encouragement: "Trust in the Lord with all your heart, and do not rely on your own insight. In all your ways acknowledge him, and he will make straight your paths" (Proverbs 3:5–6, RSV).

Because of God's love and faithfulness shown through so many people, I am a living, breathing, walking, and talking miracle, who has been given a second chance and a new life.

Dear Lord,

We love you and praise you. Life is full of trials and difficulties. Loss is so frightening, but you command us to be strong and courageous. Your word promises us that you will never leave nor forsake us. You tell us to rejoice in all of our circumstances. Help us to be obedient to you and to trust you during the darkest days and to give you praise for being with us. Thank you for your Son, Jesus, who knows our struggles and reminds us that he has overcome everything we face. In his precious and strong name we pray. Amen.

You, Lord, Are the One Whom I Have Believed

Judy K. Davidson

With *You* in the Now,
I neither have to grieve over the past nor fear the future.
All committed to *You*—
I can rest in *You* and enjoy the
abundant life of peace and joy.
In *You*, who are *light* and *life*,
I can stay energized and keep trying rather
than becoming tired and giving up.
Because *You Are*,
Anytime I feel overwhelmed, I will
say "Help me, Lord Jesus,"

And there *You* are with your hand
lifting me out of despair.
Your Spirit speaks to my spirit—
And with gratitude and joy I am able to
see that each experience of life
Strengthens my faith in *You*, my hope
in *You*, and my love for *You*.
You, Lord, are the one whom I have believed.
Like Paul, I am persuaded that *You* are able
to keep that which I have committed
until that glorious day.

What's the Worst?

Jean Mahaffey

I sat staring at the doctor with my mouth hanging open. I remember deliberately closing my lips together, too late to mask my total shock at the words that had just come out of his mouth. I looked at him, and could see the shock registered on his own face as he read, silently, the report of a PET (Positron Emission Tomography) scan on my husband Paul's brain. He had just been smiling, saying, "if there had been any problem with the scan I'm sure I would have called…" and then he fell silent. Finally, in a small voice, staring at the page in front of him and not at me or Paul, he said, "and this shows he *does* have Alzheimer's."

As a health care professional, I have delivered bad news. I have never failed to look my patient in the eye, to offer a comforting touch, and never referred to my patient in the third person as though he were in another state. "Well," I responded with an edge in my voice that many of my co-workers would have quickly recognized as trouble, "I'm glad you read the report and decided there was nothing in there we needed to know." (The PET scan was done five weeks prior.) The doctor jumped out of his chair, mumbled something about getting prescriptions, and hurried out the door. Paul looked at me, "What did all that mean?"

My heart sank to my stomach. This man who had never known a sick day in his life, this man who had stuck with me through ten years of serious health issues, this man who counted on me to explain medical issues—my man—was seriously ill. How did I explain that his doctor had just handed him a death sentence as casually as I would have purchased a ham at the grocery store. We talked quietly for a few minutes, the doctor returned to the room, handed *me* a prescription and said, "You two have plans to make, things to think about, bring him back in six months." Over my dead body was ringing somewhere in my mind, but never made it to my lips, probably the first miracle.

Paul was in shock. We had come in separate cars, and I suggested he come home with me. We could send someone for his car. No, he was going to work. He is a worker; he felt safe at work. I offered to come with him. He said no. I went home alone; he went to work alone.

When I got home, I was fuming. I was still seething at the cavalier attitude of that doctor. I went upstairs to my sanctuary, took out my Bible, and continued to fume. I wasn't just angry at the doctor; I was angry at God. How could he do this to someone who never hurt a single person in his entire life? The next morning I wrote in my prayer journal, "What kind of trick is this, God?"

I don't know how God answers your questions or speaks to you, but for me, I have found that God finds the direct approach works well. He usually responds almost immediately and in short concise sentences. Sometimes he seems to be standing next to me. My personality is not calm; it is direct, quick, and, yes, pushy and sometimes blunt. God deals with me in like terms, except he is usually very calm. Once, sitting on the ground under a tree in the backyard of our mountain vacation home, I looked across the mountains, and said, "I can feel you here, Lord". He answered immediately, "I am here, Jean, and I want you here too. Come, bring Paul. This is your home." Two months later, Paul was diagnosed with Alzheimer's. I knew what I had to do. God had prepared me.

Eleven months passed before we began to "make our move." I prayed daily for God's direction, to lead me to what I needed to do next. His answer was consistent, "Leave it all to me." One of the things that made the decision to move difficult was the birth of our first granddaughter. What a joy she was to us. By the time we finally left Georgia, she was walking. I watched her play with her granddaddy and wondered how much he would be able to remember about their time together as she grew up.

I felt lost and alone. I felt I had no one with whom to share my pain and my heartache. Friends, who had always been so dear to me, were suddenly strangers because Paul was insistent that no one be told the truth of his illness. Somewhere, in all of this, I realized that my best friend was Paul, and this time, I couldn't share my feelings with him. I prayed more and slowly felt the pull back to God. I was having trouble seeing what God was doing for me, how was he helping, where was he in the middle of this? We were truly struggling, and I couldn't see God *handling it*. I was drowning, and God was watching.

On the morning of March 1, 2009, we were ready. It was Sunday, but we had not been to church in months. I was doing all of the driving by now, and Sunday mornings were fairly quiet going through Atlanta. Our SUV was loaded to the gills. The neighbor across the street came over to ask us to reconsider and leave another day. Snow was predicted that day. Snow in the south is dangerous. He brought his three beautiful children over to say good-bye. They had recently lost their mother, and I felt like I was taking something else from them. Thirty minutes before we pulled out it began to snow.

Our son called, wait until tomorrow, please. But no, God said go today. I couldn't believe I was listening to that still small voice, but I did. He said "you need to go now; I have something to show you."

We headed north, away from Columbus, Georgia, and everything we had ever known as home. Around Pine Mountain, Georgia, we discussed turning back. I was firm; Paul was game. We drove on. We merged onto I-85 from I-185 headed to Atlanta, and the snow became heavier. There was enough traffic on the road to make the ice turn to slush. My heart was in my throat; this was dangerous, I decided. As we crossed a bridge on the interstate, an 18 wheeler flew by us on the left. In his wake, the driver covered my windshield with a thick coat of slush—total white out. In the time it takes the wipers to cross the windshield, I heard God say "Trust Me." I truly followed his instructions, wheels straight, and eyes straight ahead. I felt the car go light, wheels spinning with no traction, as our SUV was lifted and pulled in the draft of the truck's trailer and then we were moving forward again. I exhaled. When the wipers cleared the windshield, the road ahead was empty. We drove on. We were on the north side of Atlanta before I realized there was no other vehicle on the road anywhere near us. Oh, there were cars on the road, but none were near us, ahead, behind, or on either side; it was like we were riding in a bubble, with God's angels clearing our path. We drove for seven hours with no other problems, stopping only for gas and lunch. Finally, we pulled up in front of our new home, safely delivered by those angels.

Monday morning, March 2, 2009, I rose early as is my custom. I like the early mornings. I pulled my Bible out of my tote bag and read Lamentations 3:21–23. I opened the drapes and looked out on a winter wonderland. I heard God say, "Welcome home."

Since that day I have read that scripture many times, but recently I found a translation that has become my daily reading:

> But there's one other thing I remember, and remembering, I keep a grip on hope: God's loyal love couldn't have run out, his merciful love couldn't have dried up. They're created new every morning. How great your faithfulness! I'm sticking with God. . .
>
> When life is heavy and hard to take, go off by yourself. Enter the silence. Bow in prayer. Don't ask questions: Wait for hope to appear. Don't run from trouble. Take it full-face. The "worst" is never the worst.
>
> Lamentations 3:21–24, 28–30 (MSG)

It has been six years since Paul's diagnosis, and I have come a long way. We have not had an easy life in North Carolina, but I have never felt alone. I have felt lonely, much sadness, but, at last, I know how to be totally dependent on God. And when I think "this is the worst", it truly isn't. Losing my God would be the worst.

The Story behind Faces by God's Paintbrush

Gloria S. Toelle

One day when I was walking and talking with God, I looked up at the sky and saw faces in all of the clouds. *Oh, how beautiful*, I thought to myself. Then a feeling came over me and God said in my thoughts, "You are going to paint faces in clouds." "Oh, I don't know if I can Lord," I said. "I will really need to study the clouds if I do." I began to study and study clouds.

One night after supper I went to my studio and God spoke again. "Paint faces in clouds." "Oh, I can't—I don't have a canvas. All I have is this huge board I was going to use for something else. Guess I will have to use it even though it is very big."

I set up with a big bucket of water and a big brush and a lot of acrylic paint in blue, white, and red. I started by putting paint on the canvas going across from top to bottom. I just slapped that paint all over the canvas and kept adding color everywhere. When I put the red paint on, it was sticking for some reason; so, I only put it in one row. Then I covered the board and turned and walked away. "Where are the faces, Lord? Show me where and how to paint them."

I turned around to look at the painting from a distance and saw faces were everywhere! I just stood in awe and humility with tears running down my face and said, "Lord, you didn't want me to paint the faces; you just wanted me to put paint on the board—you painted in the faces."

The next morning I called my sister and told her about the painting. She said, "I have a very strong feeling to tell you to photograph the picture right now." I asked why, what was the rush? She said she did not know but that was the message she was getting. My husband photographed the painting that day and it was a very good thing. Without that picture, I would never have realized the enormity of what God had added to the painting.

My friend Cathy, who helped me clean every two weeks, came that very day. My painting was in my studio and ordinarily she would not have seen it. I showed her the photo my husband had taken and told her that I had looked everywhere but could not see a cross. I explained I felt that if God had painted the picture, a cross would be in it somewhere. She took the photo to study while I went to get a cup of coffee for us. When I returned, she said, "I see a cross and Jesus is on it." She had turned the picture sideways and there it was! So I told her that if God had painted something on two sides, maybe we should look at the other two. That is when we found the wolves, shepherd, and the horses.

I was so excited and felt I needed to make prints so others would be able to see God's work. The print company assured me they could have the prints ready for my art show in December. But as time for the show drew near, the prints were not ready. I went to the shop to see the man who had promised me he could meet my deadline. I was quite angry and told him how disappointed and upset I was with his company. That night I dreamed that God came to me and told me to go back to the man and apologize for my angry words. I questioned him because I felt justified in being upset. God told me, "My Painting, My Time."

The next day I went back to the print shop and apologized. The man was so astonished at my behavior that he confided in me, "I did not think God was real until I met you." I told him the story of the painting and why I was so anxious about the prints being ready. He told me about himself and his life and his struggles. He said that he wanted his child and future wife to be Christians and that he wanted to go to church.

It was a very humbling experience to see that God had used my apology to bring a man (perhaps a family) to him. If I had not been obedient, I would have really missed a blessing. That young man brought his fiancé and son to the art show to meet me. I was so happy to hear that they were going to a church and planned to join.

Well, I did not get the prints until about six months later. (God's timing.) When I went to get them, they were given to me in a group. And then I noticed that there were other stacks of them against the wall. I asked the man if those weren't also for me. He said that those were not part of my order; the printer had made a mistake and printed twice as many as I had requested. I asked how much money would the extras cost and he went to find out. He returned with two men and they proceeded to load them in my car. "Wait," I said. "How much do they cost? I may not be able to pay for all of those." He leaned over and softly said, "Nothing, they are all yours."

All I can say is that this is God's Painting, God's Timing, and God's printing order—double.

The following is my explanation of how to find the *faces*:

This painting has four sides. The first side I call, *The Promise.* There are a lot of faces on this side. The names of a few that have been revealed to me are Abraham, Sarah, Hagar, Mary and baby Jesus. The first three faces are from left to right across the top in the white area. Mary and baby Jesus are in the right bottom corner. Out of the body of baby Jesus, it looks like water is flowing.

Rotate the picture to the left. This side I named, *The Gift.* Here there are three views of Jesus on the cross. In one you see him face on and the other two are side views. One of the side views is as large as the face-on, but the other one is much smaller and much clearer. All are in the white area where the red, the blood, goes across the sky.

Rotate the picture left again. This side I call *The Shepherd.* In the middle of the picture is a big white spot, a lake. Behind the lake are sheep and to the left in the white area, the face of a shepherd is seen with a long stick. Above his head are three wolves. In the upper right-hand corner is a large head of Jesus wearing the crown of thorns and his blood is running from the thorns.

Rotate the picture to left again. This side I named, *Revelations.* If you look in the top right-hand corner, there are three white horses. The largest of the white horses has a rider on it. The big black spot on the left is a black horse.

Rotate to the left again and the picture is back in its original position—just the way I painted it. I did not try to draw any faces on this painting; and it has not had any additions since I prayed for God to show me the faces—I just slapped color on the four by six feet canvas board to get started. I had to name the painting *Faces by God's Paintbrush* because I know that *God* painted in the faces not me.

Faces by God's Paintbrush

Callaway Azalea Path

"I am leaving you with a gift—peace of mind and heart! And the peace I give isn't fragile like the peace the world gives. So don't be troubled or afraid."

John 14:27 (The Living Bible)

Old Covered Bridge

"The grass withers, the flowers fade, but the Word of our God shall stand forever."

Isaiah 40:8 (The Living Bible)

Day Lilies

"Consider the lilies of the field, how they grow; they neither toil nor spin; yet I tell you, even Solomon in all his glory was not arrayed like one of these."

Matthew 6:28-29 (RSV)

Whitetail Deer

"As the deer pants for streams of water, so my soul pants for you, my God."

Psalm 42:1 (NIV)

Reflections

"Be still and know that I am God."

Psalm 46:10 (NIV)

Crowing Rooster

"Let everything that has breath praise the Lord."

Psalm 150:6 (NIV)

The Okefenokee Swamp

"God is light; in him there is no darkness at all. If we walk in the light, as he is in the light, we have fellowship with one another, and the blood of Jesus, his son, purifies us from all sin."

1 John 1:5-7 (NIV

Lighthouse

"God is our refuge and strength, an ever present help in trouble. Therefore we will not fear, though the earth give way and the mountains fall into the heart of the sea, though its waters roar and foam and the mountains quake with their surging."

Psalm 46:1-3 (NIV)

Jesus on the Cross

The Story behind Jesus on the Cross

Gloria S. Toelle

A few years ago Gloria and her husband, Richard, went to the Atlanta Civic Center to see a performance of the Passion Play. She was very moved while watching the actor who betrayed Jesus on the cross. He was hanging on the cross with his head bowed with blood dripping from the crown of thorns down onto the floor. There was a spotlight behind him illuminating his shoulders and coming across his head. Gloria told herself that she wanted to paint that image; and so the next morning she began.

She got a canvas and began painting using acrylics. She worked using multiple colors and then she re-wet her brush and began to *pull-out* the figure of Jesus. Lastly, she added the light that illuminated Jesus' bowed head and shoulders. Notice that there is no ethnicity visible and that we do not see Jesus' face. The figure could be any adult male of any race. The message is that Jesus died for *everyone*.

Buddha or Jesus?
A Tale of Two Women

Judy K. Davidson

Kim, one of my dear friends, was born and grew up in Vietnam. She and all of her family members were Buddhists just like the great majority of the Vietnamese people. Kim married an American GI, moved to the United States, and became a naturalized citizen. Through three decades of living in the US, Kim was introduced to Christianity by various family and friends. She politely listened and even attended church services; but at home she kept her Buddhist shrine, burned incense, and followed the teachings of Buddha.

Kim has two jobs: she works full-time in Civil Service at our local Army base and part-time as a nail technician.

Many of my friends are also her customers; we all love her. She has a sweet spirit and is one of the kindest people I know. She is also very intelligent, has a large dose of common sense, and knows more about politics than many Americans born in this country. Because I see her every two weeks, I have been able to watch her gradual acceptance of the Christian life. Very recently she said, "I was a Buddhist for fifty eight years and then I gave my life to Christ." I asked her to tell me her story and she gave me permission to share it with you.

A year or so before her conversion, Kim began to feel a real pull toward Jesus. She told me one day that she knew Jesus was the Son of God, but she still followed Buddha. Friends would invite her to church and she would agree to go. Three different times she got up and dressed on Sunday mornings and drove to the church. And then she just sat in her car either unwilling or unable to get out and go in to the service. Finally she would drive herself back home.

About that time, a Vietnamese Baptist church was started with a minister driving down from Atlanta every Sunday. Friends invited Kim to attend with them and she said she would go. She told me, "They would have church and then have a real Vietnamese luncheon afterwards. I went to church so I could eat Vietnamese food. I am not a great cook and that food kept me going each Sunday."

Finally there came a week when no lunch was going to be served. Kim struggled with whether she would go or not; all week she kept having a feeling that she must attend. That Sunday she got up, got dressed, and arrived a good bit early. As in days before, she just sat in her car. Across the street was a fast-food restaurant. "I told myself, maybe I can go over there to get something to eat and the line will be long; and by the time my food comes and I eat, it will be too late for church." So she walked across the street to order her food. "I went in and there was no one in line. My food was ready in about three minutes. Even though I ate slowly, I still had five minutes left before church started. It only took less than a minute to walk back across the street; so it looked like I had to go to church."

Kim reluctantly went into the service. All during that hour, she kept having a "feeling go all over me" to speak to the pastor and give her life to Christ. But even when he gave an altar call, Kim did not go down front. She felt a real need to speak to the pastor because she also felt that she had a word for him from the Holy Spirit. After the service, she stayed back as the other people were leaving so she could speak to the pastor in private. "I don't know what this means," she said, "but I am supposed to tell you not to give up." He looked at her incredulously and said, "What?" She repeated her statement that he was not to give up and the pastor began to cry. He said, "You have been sent to me by God. I was going to resign because I felt that the church was not growing under my ministry. I have had some personal problems and have been praying to seek God's direction about what to do. This is my answer." Then Kim shared her struggles and with the pastor's help, she prayed that her sins be forgiven. And Jesus came into her heart and she became in dwelled by the Holy Spirit. "I am a Christian!"

She has become a spirit-filled Christian woman who boldly speaks about her faith. One of her dear friends to whom she has ministered is named Kristy: a woman with a past much like Kim's. Kristy is also a Vietnamese woman, raised a Buddhist, came to the United States, and owns a nail salon. Kristy, too, felt the pull of Christ but was very reluctant to leave her Buddhist upbringing. She was occasionally attending Kim's Vietnamese church and over time she came to know that she wanted to give her life to Jesus.

She decided to go one particular Sunday and answer the altar call when it was given. However, that morning she woke up with her back in spasms; she could not get out of bed without her husband's help. She said to him, "I want to go to church today but I cannot even walk." He said, "Why don't you pray to Jesus and ask him to take your pain away?" *Okay.* Kristy thought to herself, *What do I have to lose?* She prayed and asked Jesus to take away her pain if he wanted her to go to church that day. And, as she later told Kim, "In just a few minutes, my pain was all gone." She dressed and walked out of her bedroom to the astonishment of her husband. He asked, "Where are you going?" She answered that she was going to church as planned. And as she wanted to, Kristy answered the altar call and gave her life to Jesus that day. Just like Kim, Kristy marks her life before and after Jesus came into her heart.

Is Jesus calling you, my friend, or someone you know? Don't give up on yourself or on another. He is only a prayer away.

> *Jesus said to her, "I am the resurrection and the life. He who believes in me will live, even though he dies; and whoever lives and believes in me will never die. Do you believe this?" "Yes, Lord," she told him, "I believe that you are the Christ, the Son of God, who was to come into the world."*

> John 11:25-27
> (NIV)

A Turning Point

Larry Coger

The Joyful Noise Sunday School Class has a Christmas Party each year. It is a wonderful time of enjoying good food and fellowship in the mood of the season that we celebrate. They find it in their hearts to give me, their teacher, a gift each year. I am humbled and appreciative of the gift, but I recognize and express to them their greater gift to me. They are kind enough to let me serve as their teacher, which requires me to rise each day and spend an hour enjoying a good cup of coffee while reading, making notes, and praying about the lesson for the week. If not for serving as the class teacher, I would probably just sleep another hour each morning and ramble my way through another day. But, since I have a highly developed fear of looking foolish on Sunday morning, I find an incentive to spend the hour each day in preparation. I have even come to the point that I look forward to the early morning sessions and feel a small void if I miss a day. This has not always been the case.

I began teaching a young adult Sunday school class shortly after college and marriage. I don't know why I started teaching. It seemed the thing to do since no one else wanted to or was willing to serve. If you know what a leisure suit is, then you recognize the era of which I speak. I probably spent an hour each week in preparation, usually on Saturday night. The classes were more of an invitation to discuss scripture than to teach what the scripture revealed about the God who created us and his son, Jesus. This pattern of teaching lasted for more years than I want to admit and I often bemoaned the task. *Why me?* I would ask myself. *Why doesn't someone else volunteer to teach the class?* Encouragement was plentiful from the class members. I wondered why. Then there was a turning point about midway of a thirty-five year teaching career when everything changed.

The series of lessons was on the topic of the Holy Spirit written by Herschel Hobbs. I was absorbed by the subject. The message was so clear. We are each given spiritual gifts by the Holy Spirit when we are born spiritually as Jesus explained to Nicodemus late one night. The gifts properly recognized, developed, and used allow the Holy Spirit to use human Christians as a conduit through which he can accomplish the purposes of God in the world. The Holy Spirit resides in human Christians and replaces in a spiritual sense the physical presence of Jesus in the world. The spiritual gifts are somewhat unique to the individual, but generally fall into certain categories and are not to be confused with talents.

During this study it became apparent to me that my spiritual gifts were teaching and discernment. I began to realize that teaching the word of God was not related to my ability. In allowing the Holy Spirit to use me and my voice, he could reveal the word of God to those who were attentive. Prior to this realization I was depending on my own ability to interpret and explain God's word, which in retrospect was foolish. I now understand why I approached each lesson with a certain amount of dread. I was relying on my own ability and not allowing the Holy Spirit to work through me. I came to understand that the Holy Spirit only needs a conduit to work through. Yes, I must study and prepare, but then I must yield control and let the Holy Spirit speak through me. This is not easy! I always feel a need to be in control, and to prepare more and study more to do an effective job. So, turning control over to the Holy Spirit was and still is difficult.

It happened slowly over time. Then one week I was busy, tired, distracted and had not prepared the lesson very well. I prayed to God, confessed my failure and asked for his help in presenting the lesson for the week. As I presented the lesson to the class, the words and thoughts flowed so smoothly that I was amazed. I had yielded control to the Holy Spirit, not willingly but by necessity, and the Holy Spirit just flowed through me like water through an open pipe. After this and several other "learning experiences", I prayed each week for the Holy Spirit to give me the words to speak, to just take control, to prepare the listener to receive the word, and to just let me be a conduit through which to work.

This prayer is answered weekly. I no longer dread the lesson time, the preparation, or the exposure of my deepest feelings. On the contrary, I look forward to the lesson time each week. I am only a conduit through which the Holy Spirit works. I have fully yielded to the Spirit's control. I don't have to worry about presenting the lesson or the impact of the lesson on those who attend. It's an amazing, even mesmerizing, experience to be used by the Spirit of God. But, I understand very clearly, it is not about me. I give all credit to the Holy Spirit working through me. The Holy Spirit calls no attention to himself, but always points to the work of Christ on the cross. Likewise, I call no attention to myself.

I also understand very clearly that the Holy Spirit cannot work through someone if they have sin in their lives for which they have not repented. Sin clogs the conduit and prevents the Holy Spirit from working through them. Daily prayer including confession, repentance, and asking for forgiveness is a necessity. A humble spirit is also critical to being used by the Holy Spirit. I pray each day that the Holy Spirit will give me the words to speak, the wisdom to understand, and to take control of the lesson presentation. Satan works diligently to oppose the work of the Holy Spirit. His primary weapon is pride, overt pride and subtle pride. If Satan can get those who yield control to the Holy Spirit to develop a sense of pride about the work of the Holy Spirit through them, he can undo a great portion of the good accomplished. Satan never rests. He must be recognized and defeated daily through prayer that beckons the power of the Holy Spirit.

The Hebrews used the word *uber* to describe the emotions of a farmer as he gazed over a bountiful crop ready for harvest. In our present day English, *uber* is the root word for exuberance, which gives some measure of meaning to the emotion described. The word expressed the farmer's inner joy that came from seeing the results of his labor. The farmer planted the seed, cultivated the field before and after planting, and tended the plants until they were ready for harvest. The farmer also recognizes that God has provided through nature's design plentiful amounts of the sunshine and water necessary to produce the abundant crop. The farmer has invested his labor in the crop, but recognizes that God has provided the bountiful crop ready for harvest.

Uber comes as close as any word I have found to describe the feeling that comes from being used by the Holy Spirit. If we prepare ourselves and allow the Holy Spirit to work through us, then we can then know what it means to be "filled with the Spirit." This experience is the greater gift that the Joyful Noise Sunday School Class gives to me.

Heavenly Father,

Forgive my sins, Lord. Forgive my unclean thoughts, my sinful acts, and my failure to act when you call on me. I repent of my sins and I ask for your forgiveness so that I may be a clean vessel through which your Holy Spirit may flow. Renew your spirit in me this day.

Give me discernment that I may hear your call. Give me courage to respond. Give me strength to act. Give me faith to rely on your spirit to minister to others through me.

For all that will be accomplished by your spirit working through me, may all glory, honor, and praise be to your holy name. I desire only to be your humble servant and a conduit through which your Holy Spirit works.

Amen

What in the World Are We Here For?

Judy K. Davidson

What in the world are we here for?
Ponder this thought for a while.
God says seek *him* first in everything,
If you would be *his* child.
What in the world are we here for?
What did Jesus do?
Humbly taking the role of a servant,
He died for me and for you.
What in the world are we here for?
What does the Bible say?
We must love and care for each other.
And don't forget to pray.

What in the world are we here for?
Brothers and sisters are we.
By working together in mission,
We build our community.
What do we *do* with this knowledge?
A new book to read then store on the shelf?
No! The gifts of the Spirit aren't given
To help me help myself!
Jesus said those who love him *obey* him.
And what did he say we should do?
Love God with all of our being and
Treat others as you wish they'd treat you.

Ministry in the Martketplace

Danny Falligant

So often when we as Christians think of ministry, we think about our work in the Church. We think about serving on committees, administrative boards, teaching Sunday School, collecting the offering, and so on and so forth. These are ministries that we generally do on Sunday morning, Sunday evening, and Wednesday night. However, Jesus made it clear that ministry is a lifestyle that we live every day.

When we think of the term minister, we think of a person, who preaches on Sundays, leads Wednesday night prayer service, has graduated from the seminary, and has been ordained. Jesus would say nothing could be further from the truth. When Jesus selected his initial team for evangelism, he chose uneducated and ordinary men, most who fished for a living. Jesus did not go to the learned religious leaders of the day. In fact, Jesus was most critical of these religious leaders.

As Jesus trained the twelve, he taught through simple stories and examples about life so that his apostles could picture the message in their minds. As Christians, we should let our life be a picture or illustration to the world of what it looks like to follow Jesus. Jesus said "follow me and I will make you fishers of men." Hopefully, as Christians, our lives would catch people's attention and introduce them to the joy of knowing Jesus personally. Jesus said to his followers that we are to be salt and light to a lost and dying world. The world needs to taste and see that Jesus is good. The world will observe this by the way Christians live, especially in the marketplace.

What is the message of the Christian as he or she goes through life on a daily basis? It is a plain and simple message of reconciliation. Paul says that God gave us the word of reconciliation, so we could pass it on by our life and our words.

> Therefore, if any man is in Christ, he is a new creature; the old things passed away; behold new things have come. Now all these things are from God, who reconciled us to Himself through Christ and gave us the ministry of reconciliation, namely

that God was in Christ reconciling the world to himself, not counting their trespasses against them and He has committed to us the word of reconciliation. Therefore, we are ambassadors for Christ, as though God were entreating through us; we beg you on behalf of Christ, be reconciled to God.

2 Corinthians 5:17–20 (NASB)

The words ministry or minister come from the Greek word *diakonia*, which means to serve in order to bring relief. The English word deacon comes from the word diakonia. As Christians our job is to serve as ministers and bring relief (the word of reconciliation) to a suffering world. The people of the world are suffering from the pain and penalty of sin and Christians have the relief needed because we have the word of reconciliation. How do we communicate this word of reconciliation? By the words we speak and the way we live. The foundation of our speech and our life should be love. Jesus said, "By this shall all men know you are my disciples, if you have love for one another" (John 13:35, NIV). Love is usually communicated by serving.

Jesus also said, "For the Son of man came not to be served but to serve and give his life a ransom for many" (Matthew 20:28, NIV). In other words, the greater the sacrifice, the greater the love. Serving others is done daily and usually at very inconsistent times. At least this has been true for me.

One day I had a lady client come to my office to sign her will. Her name was Patricia, and we were in grammar school together. She was a feisty lady in her fifties whose vocabulary was very colorful. She had been through a divorce and was filled with bitterness. In addition to the divorce, she had a terrible childhood and she needed relief. Sitting at the conference table in my office, I simply asked her, "Now that you have made provisions for the disposition of your worldly assets, what provisions have you made for stepping into eternity?" Her answer surprised me. She said she was glad I had asked her that question. I was expecting her to reject my inquiry. Patricia was suffering with cancer and she knew stepping into eternity could be sooner rather than later. Patricia said she had called her priest several weeks ago and he had not returned her call. I told her that I was not an ordained priest, but that I could be a priest (God's messenger) to her that day. I shared with Patricia the Gospel message of the death, burial, and resurrection of Jesus. Patricia admitted she was a sinner and that she needed to be reconciled to God by accepting Jesus as her savior. Patricia prayed to accept Jesus by faith and be adopted into God's family.

That day Patricia became a new creature in Christ. The next day, my wife, Carol, bought her a Bible. As Patricia read the scriptures, she experienced the love of God as she learned about forgiveness and freedom from the bonds of sin.

Patricia was in a Tuesday night ladies dinner club. The transformation of Patricia's life became evident as each week she would share with her friends the joy of personally knowing Jesus as her savior. The ladies could see and hear the new excitement Patricia had for life even though she was suffering with terminal cancer. Patricia now knew about her future and the joy of eternity waiting for her.

Patricia died about six months after coming to my office. She had given me written instructions about handling her eulogy. The attendance at her funeral was standing room only.

Her priest shared that Patricia was saved through participating in religious ritual. I had the opportunity to say "Patricia was trusting in the blood of Jesus for a personal relationship with God." I used Patricia's Bible to share her eulogy. I have never seen so many sticky notes in a Bible— marking her favorite verses. Patricia's testimony spoke volumes to her friends and relatives the day of her funeral. Patricia only had six months to live the life of reconciliation, but what joy she experienced in those months. During that time she truly was salt and light to those who came in contact with her.

I share this story with you because some forty years ago, I became a Christian by studying the Bible to teach Sunday School. As a result of my decision to follow Jesus, I viewed my law practice more as a ministry rather than a means of making a living. Over the years, I have had the privilege of sharing my faith and praying with clients in my office, the marketplace. Often, I have had the opportunity to weep with those who weep and rejoice with those who rejoice.

There are many Patricias in our lives that need our daily availability for weeping and rejoicing.

> Dear Father,
>
> I pray that I will be faithful to obey your call daily when you bring opportunities across my path to be a minister to someone in the marketplace. Help me to realize that the Christian life is about serving others. I know that as I serve others in Jesus' name, I am serving you. Amen

My Angel Policeman

Judy K. Davidson

A few years ago, I had foot surgery in February. My husband and I usually go to the beach in May and my doctor had given me the okay for that year. The skin on my foot had healed, but I still wore the big air boot for stability and protection. Also, my foot swelled and was quite painful whenever it wasn't elevated. Walking and standing were really uncomfortable.

The morning of the day we were to leave for our trip started off just fine. My husband left for work to be in a conference all morning and planned to be home about 1 p.m. I promised him I would be ready and waiting. By 11 a.m., I was packed and ready to leave, so I decided to treat myself to lunch from one of my favorite local places. Off I went with time to spare. The parking lot was almost full and the only spot left was quite a distance from the restaurant. Just as I was parking my car, one of my sisters called me on my cell phone. I sat in the car for a few minutes chatting with her before going in to order my lunch. Even though it was early May, it was already pretty hot; I left my windows down a little and that turned out to be a very good thing.

I ordered and paid for my takeout and started walking or should I say limping back to my car. As I limped along, I was searching in my purse for my car keys and fussing to myself, "I can't ever find anything in this dumb purse. Everything always winds up in the bottom and I can't see because the inside is black." Just as I reached my car door, I looked inside and there on the console sat my car keys. I must have removed them while on the phone and put them down. I tried all four car doors just in case but they were locked up tight. So I limped back to the sidewalk to sit down on a bench in the shade. There were a spare set of keys at my house—I just needed someone to help me.

I called my secretary hoping she could come and take me home to get the keys; good plan but she was out to lunch. I called my mother who lived just a couple of miles from my house. I hoped she could just go by my house, get the keys and bring them to me. She was home and was willing to help except she was waiting for the plumber—could I wait an hour or so? I told her I would call her back if I didn't get anyone else. I couldn't call my husband; he was in the conference.

So there I sat with my foot swelling. I prayed and asked God to help me think of someone to call. No one came to mind. And then I prayed again and said, "Lord, if there was just a policeman, he could help me open my car." The words just finished going across my mind when a policeman pulled into the parking lot and parked right next to my car! I jumped up and limped as fast as I could to get to him. I told him my dilemma and he saw my keys on the console. "Ma'am, he said, this is not a regular police cruiser. This is a crime scene investigation vehicle and doesn't have a lock opener in it. But if we had a clothes hanger, I think we could open your door."

There was Gold's Gym in the shopping center and I suggested maybe they would have a hanger. Well, the two of us went over to the gym; he was briskly walking and I was by now sort of hopping along. We went in and asked the young woman at the desk if she had a hanger. "I don't think so. Our members provide their own things and there are hooks in the lockers." She started looking under the counter and suddenly said, "Wow, here is a hanger. We just have this one. This must be your lucky day." We thanked her and headed back to my car.

After the policeman untwisted the hanger to make it

straight, he began trying to push the lock open. You see, the locks on my car are not the push down-pull up kind with the knobs. Mine are the kind that you press in to lock and unlock. When he started working on the lock, I moved to the passenger's side of the car to give him plenty of room. Every time he tried to open the lock, the hanger would just bend. It was not rigid enough to apply the amount of pressure needed to open the lock. I could hear him talking under his breath saying, "Come on. Please, let this work."

I put my head down on the car and prayed again. "Lord, you sent me a policeman and gave us a hanger. Please help us figure out how to open this door." As I lifted my head, I saw my car antenna right by my hand. I quickly unscrewed it and asked if it would work. He smiled and took the antenna and had my door open in seconds. I thanked him and asked if I could pay him. He said, "Oh no, Ma'am. Helping the Public is my job." I said the least I could do was to buy his lunch and tried to give him mine but he just politely refused. "You are an angel God sent my way today," I told him. He said helping was his pleasure and then he got into his car and drove away. He drove away!

He did not go into any of the three restaurants or the gym or the drugstore or any other store. He just drove off. His involvement in the episode probably took ten to twelve minutes, really not too much time. But since he did not go into any store, why had he come into the parking lot just as I prayed for a policeman? Why had he found a place to park next to my car? Why did the gym just happen to have a hanger when they don't provide them? Why, why, why?

The policeman appeared because God sent me an angel that day. Blessings don't happen by chance or by accident. They come completely by divine design.

And guess what? I was home, fed, and even rested by the time my husband came in from work. I even had a great story to tell him on the way to the beach.

> *Dear Father,*
>
> *Thank you for allowing us to pray to you about anything that concerns us. Thank you that we can come to you whenever—we don't have to call and make an appointment; we don't have to wait for a certain time; we are not limited to just a few minutes of your time. We can talk as much or as little as we want. We can also just say, "Father" and you know exactly what we need and feel without explanation. You are so kind to us and faithful to your word. Please grant us the wisdom to pray to you at all times, in all circumstances, and with all kinds of prayers.*
>
> *In the name of our Lord and Savior, Jesus, we pray. Amen*

If You Leave God, It Is Your Choice

Mike Cavin

About twenty-two years ago my wife was diagnosed with cancer. We had been married twelve years and had three small children. I knew nowhere else to turn; I decided to turn to God, and discovered he was there, and had never turned away from me. At that crucial time, my favorite passage of scripture became Romans 8:31–39.

The first verse contains a thought-provoking question: "If God is for us, who is against us" (Romans 8:31, NASB)? When events happen in our lives, we too often give both God and the devil too much blame or credit. When things happen that we didn't expect, we ask God, "Why did you let that happen?" Or when we do something bad and discover regret, we cry out like the Flip Wilson character, "The devil made me do it!" The truth of the matter is that part of the reality of creation is order, life, and death. God is not a puppeteer simply pulling strings on our lives and making us dance like marionettes. He decided to give us free will and sometimes we choose wrongly. I believe the truth, that whenever God is on our team, there is no force that can overcome us. There are events in life that will shock us and cause us to stagger and stumble. There are waves that will rock the boat but nothing that will overcome us. If our ship sinks, we are usually the ones that helped bring the water on board.

Verse 35 begins, "Who will separate us from the love of Christ" (Romans: 8:35, NASB)? Whenever a relationship breaks down, someone must choose to walk away. Sometimes that is the right decision. No person ought to remain in an abusive relationship. If you are being abused, you ought to get out of that relationship as quickly and as safely as possible.

I am a United Methodist and we do not vote members in or out of our churches as part of our normal policy. So, when someone leaves a United Methodist Church, that person usually has chosen to walk away—perhaps for a variety of reasons. But, the person chooses to leaves; the Church remains—it does not go anywhere. My love for my children is not based on what they do or don't do. They will always be my children and I will always love them even if I don't love what they do. So it is with God's love: God will not leave us; however, tragically, sometimes we walk away from God.

I used to just *hope* that Verses 38 and 39 were true. I hoped that I would never lose God when the challenges of life used came my way. Because, God walked with me through those long years of my wife's illness and suffering, I now *know* that these verses are indeed true. They say,

> For I am convinced that neither death, nor life, nor angels, nor principalities, nor things present, nor things to come, nor powers, nor height, nor depth, nor any other created thing, will be able to separate us from the love of God, which is in Christ Jesus our Lord.
>
> Romans 8:38–39 (NASB)

Cancer is an awful disease that has touched most families today in one way or another. Some have great stories of healing and overcoming the disease. Others have been caught off guard and death has come with unexpected quickness. Even though healing has been sought and at times even claimed, the cancer may recur. When a person hears "the cancer has returned", shock and disappointment become the adjectives that describe life. What cancer has taught me is that this terrible disease does not have to separate me from God. My wife fought a valiant fight against cancer for sixteen years before it took over her body completely; she died the day before our twenty-eighth anniversary. In that struggle, I learned that God never left us. Never once were we cut off from God or his people.

As a United Methodist pastor, I served several local churches during much of the time my wife was ill. A few years before her death my job changed; I was assigned to be a District Superintendent which means I oversaw several pastors and their churches. That new job removed my family from the closeness of a regular congregation; and yet, even in this change, God never let us go. We were loved, nurtured, and prayed for by the congregations of many churches. Life and death brought challenges, pain, suffering, and grief but *never* separation from God.

Not only did God never leave us, but he kept us close and opened new doors of caring and renewal. I am so grateful to be a Christian and part of the community of faith that is willing to walk with me through dark places. I am so glad to believe without a doubt in the resurrection and life eternal. As hard as life and death are when one walks with Christ, I cannot imagine a life without Christ and the community of faith walking beside me.

God not only walks with us through the dark places but he helps us return to the high places of life. At just the right time, God brought into my life another wonderful, spirit-filled Christian woman. We have now been married for four years. She has helped joy to return to my life and let my grief be healed. God does not always give me what I want, but he has always given me what I needed. When what I needed was new life and joy, he brought that to me.

I have walked with God through some dark days. I am now walking in light again. I just can't imagine walking anywhere without him. Throughout my life, God has never left me; and, because of that, I will never leave him.

Dear God,

Thank you for continuing to walk with me. Forgive me for the times I only see you on sunny days. Thank you for the assurance that you are always with me and that you never have and never will leave me alone.

Help me to turn to you more quickly on the cloudy days and see your light as the pathway through to brighter days. You have never left me and I will never leave you. Thank you. Amen.

Still Looking for Grace

Chuck Bradshaw

The kennel has been empty for about a month. The concrete floor is littered with the evidence of changing seasons. An occasional squirrel, finally daring to step into the wire confines that would have meant certain death a few months ago, scavenges for hickory nuts. The red wasps buzz. The birds chirp. The breeze makes a gentle rustling among the trees. But the kennel is quiet.

She seemed almost indestructible. She was a great running partner for years. She kept the other neighborhood dogs away but then tried to trip me by getting too close to my feet. She enjoyed chasing things with no regard to their size. It was during an apparent deer-chasing episode that she got tangled up in barbed wire and eventually lost a back leg. But for Grace, that was only a minor setback.

Almost three years ago, she underwent surgery for cancer. She was not supposed to live more than six months. She was a survivor.

She enjoyed getting her belly rubbed and especially being scratched on the side where her leg was missing. She hid in her Dogloo during storms and relaxed in a clump of prickly Spanish bayonet plants other times.

She breathed her last with that big old head resting on my leg, while I scratched her side and spoke softly to her. I buried her where the kids' tree house used to be. I cut down the tallest Spanish bayonet and planted it in that spot. I think Grace would approve.

I still find myself looking for her. When I step out into the back yard in the morning, I look toward the kennel. When I come up the driveway in the afternoon, that's the first place I look. When I park my truck and climb out, I've caught myself more than once starting to yell, "Yo, Grace."

As sweet as she was, she also was dumb as a post. That may explain why someone put her out and left her years ago. She wandered up on our place and adopted us. We named her Grace. We hadn't asked for her. At first, we did not want her. We even tried to get rid of her. She simply refused to leave. "Grace"—what an appropriate name.

Years ago, someone asked me, "Does that bulldog belong to you?" "Not really," I responded. "I belong to her."

What seemingly was true then about a three-legged dog is patently true about God's grace. Grace is God's unmerited favor. It is, in fact, favor in the place of what we really deserve as sinners. Most Christians at least give lip service to the truth that it was God's grace in Christ that brought them into relationship with him. Yet, many of us live as if now we're "on our own." We forget, or perhaps we never learned, that our ongoing relationship with God is based on grace just as much as is our salvation. This is not a new problem. It is as old as humanity.

A favorite story that Jesus told was that of a father and his two sons. The younger son insisted that his dad give him his inheritance early. Upon receiving it, he left home, squandered his money and soon found himself in dire straits. Jesus tells us what the boy was thinking:

> How many of my father's hired men have food to spare, and here I am starving to death! I will set out and go back to my father and say to him: Father, I have sinned against heaven and against you. I am no longer worthy to be called your son; make me like one of your hired men.

> Luke 15:17-19 (NIV)

The father welcomed him back with open arms. But his older brother was livid. Jesus tells us what the angry sibling said:

Look! All these years I've been slaving for you and never disobeyed your orders. Yet you never gave me even a young goat so I could celebrate with my friends. But when this son of yours who has squandered your property with prostitutes comes home, you kill the fattened calf for him!

Luke 15:29-30 (NIV)

The younger was convinced that he had to earn his way back. The older was convinced that his dutiful obedience already had earned his place for him. *Both* boys were wrong. God's grace cannot be earned. It is free. The apostle Paul reminded his fellow believers in Galatia about the necessity of continuing in grace. "I would like to learn just one thing from you: Did you receive the Spirit by observing the law, or by believing what your heard? Are you so foolish? After beginning with the Spirit, are you now trying to attain your goal by human effort?" (Galatians 3:2-3, NIV).

Because we are rational creatures, God intends for us to use our minds. We need to think carefully—and Biblically. Living by faith means living without scheming. That means we need to keep our spiritual eyes open and watch for the Lord. No matter how difficult the day, no matter how late the hour, it is honoring to God for us to be found still looking for grace.

Merciful Lord,

Thank you for your marvelous grace found in Christ. In a world where I constantly am bombarded with affirmations such as, 'You deserve the best," and "Enjoy it. You earned it," help me to remember that such sentiments, while mostly well-intentioned, simply are not true. The truth is all that I am, all that I have, and all that the future holds for me is dependent upon your grace. You who began a good work in me will one day complete it – and in the same way. "Tis grace hath brought me safe thus far, and grace will lead me home."

Amen.

White Dishes

Judy K. Davidson

In 2005, Hurricane Katrina lambasted through the Gulf of Mexico and slammed into huge portions of Louisiana and Mississippi. Greater than thirty feet of saltwater ruined beaches, buildings, and the way of life for thousands of people. Winds of 125–150 miles per hour easily removed homes, cars, and businesses; many of the survivors lost everything they owned. When it became evident that leaving the area was the only solution, some moved West and North. And very many came East and stopped temporarily or permanently in our southwestern city in Georgia.

In the weeks following the entrance of the displaced persons to our city, many public and private groups opened shelters. My United Methodist Church opened a "household" bank from which persons could get new or gently used kitchen items, furniture, and clothes. The bank was open several hours per day and church members were asked for items to give to the bank and for volunteers to work. Our church members were generous and got very busy filling up the bank. But the need often emptied the bank in just a few days; every Sunday there was a new appeal for more items, especially things that are necessary to set up housekeeping when a family has nothing.

Permit me to take a sidetrack here and tell you about a Bible study I had recently attended on *The Workbook on the Seven Deadly Sins* by Maxie Dunnam and Kimberly Dunnam Reisman. My ideas on the seven sins changed quite a bit during this study. I had started the study knowing that *pride* was something I dealt with on a continuing basis. The Bible says that, "Pride goes before destruction, and a haughty spirit before a fall" (Proverbs 16:18, rsv). I was quite humbled to understand that I actually had committed (and was committing) *all seven* of the sins. You see, we learned from this study that there are degrees of sin and each sin has several other names. Let's take greed for example. I had never considered myself *greedy*, but the Dunnam/Reisman book showed me that hoarding is a type of greed. Hoarding in this sense is having something and not using it—just hanging on to the item because it "might come in handy" one of these days. Especially is this hoarding, *greed*, when someone else could make good use of the hoarded item.

Let's get back to the Katrina refugees. One particular Sunday, Brad, our youth minister made a special appeal to restock the household bank because there was going to be an influx of new people that week. I immediately had a message in my head that said, "White dishes." Oh, not my white dishes! I loved those dishes—they were white pottery with a raised grapevine and clusters of grapes around the border. I had purchased them for nearly nothing when one of our department stores was going out of business. The dinner plates were a dollar each, salad plates and bowls were 75 cents and the mugs were 50 cents. I bought ten place settings for just $30! I knew they would look so pretty at Christmas, Valentines' Day, the Fourth of July, etc. Well, they would look pretty, but I had bought them about two years previously and had only used them once. But no matter, surely God would not expect me to donate my white dishes?

I had a thought: *Ask Don* (my husband). So I said, "Don, do you care if I donate our beautiful white dishes to the outreach bank?" And my *precious darling* said, "What white dishes?" That really wasn't the response I was after. So, I went to work and culled through all of my kitchen items; every time I had two of something, one went into the donate pile. When I was through, I thought I had a respectable amount to donate. Again I heard, "White dishes." Reluctantly I said, "Okay, Lord. Thy will not mine." And I went—obediently but not joyfully—into the dining room and packed my white dishes.

Monday morning on the way to work I went by the donation center. Just as predicted, there were many displaced people waiting to go in. I walked in with my kitchen items, some curtains, and some clothes; the people in the room swooped down on my used things like they were something really special. Then I brought in the first of the two boxes with the dishes. There was an older lady and two younger women looking at all the donated things; when I put down the box, the older lady asked if she could look inside. I said, "Sure, this is a box of dishes and I am going to get another one from my car." When I came back inside, she looked at me in astonishment and said, "Ma'am, are you really giving away these beautiful plates and things?" I said that I was. And she asked how many there were. I told her ten place settings. She looked at me again, this time with even more awe and said, "Honey, do you know that there are ten of us in our family?"

Very humbly I shook my head. *Honey* hadn't known about the family of ten; but God did. He knew before I ever bought those white dishes that I would need to give them away. I learned a lot about obedience that morning. I also learned on a deeper level how kind God is. You see, I could have taken all of my things to the shelter and never learned anything about the needs of the recipients. God did not owe me an explanation about *why* I should take those dishes to donate—he could have merely said, "Because I told you to!" But in his magnificent kindness, he allowed me to see a glimpse of his planning. What a blessing! Who knew a woman could learn so much about our loving, Heavenly Father from a bunch of white dishes?

Dear Father,

Please forgive me that you often have to practically drag me kicking and screaming toward the blessings that you have for me. I am sorry that I am not always instantly obedient when I know you are leading me in a certain way. I ask you for guidance and then respond with a begrudging attitude. That is not the way a true Christian behaves. I want to be that obedient woman after your own heart. Please accept my gratitude for your patience. I do love you so. Amen

Benediction

Surely God is my salvation; I will trust and not be afraid. The LORD, the LORD, is my strength and my song; he has become my salvation.

Isaiah 12:2 (NIV)

Now to Him who is able to keep you from stumbling, and to present you faultless before the presence of His glory with exceeding joy, to God our Savior, who alone is wise, be glory, majesty, dominion and power, both now and forever.

Jude: 24–25 (NIV)

About the author

Judy K. Davidson is a Christian who enjoys learning and teaching the Word. She has served in various capacities in her local church and has taught children and adults in Sunday school, Bible school, and Bible studies. She also enjoys singing alto in her church choir. Judy recently retired as a nurse educator after a career of forty-one years. She and her husband, Don, have two children and six grandsons. They live in the country in western central Georgia.

About The Illustrator

Gloria Toelle expresses her love for art in a multitude of media. A native of Columbus, Georgia, she studied with a number of well-known artists to develop these various disciplines. Geri Davis guided her in oils, watercolors, and pen and ink. Ralph Taylor gave her more instruction in watercolors and she studied with Milton Lenoir for acrylics. Not surprisingly, she invested most of her tutorials studying the intricacies of China Painting including portraits, design and raised paste, carving and painting with gold with the likes of Jane Marcks, Celee Evens, Stephen Hayes, Barbara Jenson, and Syra Hansen.

While she applies her talent in oils, acrylics, watercolor, pastels, pencil, pen and ink, and pottery, she is best known for her award winning China paintings. She was awarded many first, second, and third place ribbons in China Painting at the Georgia National Fair during the years 2006-2012. She also won a Merchant Award at the

Columbus Artists' Guild Members show in 2007 with one of her large China paintings.

She was a member of the Columbus Porcelain Guild and served as President 2001-2. She is a member of the Columbus Artists' Guild, the Pine Mountain Porcelain Guild in Pine Mountain, Georgia, and the National Porcelain Guild of the World.

Gloria is a regular participant in local art shows and events in Georgia. Her work is displayed and for sale in a local gallery, The Joseph House Art Gallery, in downtown Columbus, Georgia.